G000038875

Hot-Ticket Meetings

Leadership Planners Series

Future-Proof Your Team

Win 'Em Over

Dynamic Discipline

Hot-Ticket Meetings

Leadership Planners

Hot-Ticket Meetings

CATHERINE HAKALA-AUSPERK

ALA Editions

CHICAGO | 2020

CATHERINE HAKALA-AUSPERK is an author, trainer, and national speaker and library consultant. She teaches at Kent State University's iSchool, for the American Library Association's Certified Public Library Administrator (CPLA) program, and for many other organizations. She is the author of many books, including *Renew Yourself: A Six-Step Plan for More Meaningful Work, Build a Great Team: One Year to Success, Be a Great Boss: One Year to Success*, and this leadership planner series. Her passions are supporting; coaching; and developing great libraries, successful teams, and—especially—strong and effective library leaders. You can follow her on Facebook at https://www.facebook.com/librariesthrive or on her website, librariesthrive.com.

© 2020 by the American Library Association

Extensive effort has gone into ensuring the reliability of the information in this book; however, the publisher makes no warranty, express or implied, with respect to the material contained herein.

ISBN: 978-0-8389-4628-2 (paper)

Library of Congress Cataloging-in-Publication Data
Names: Hakala-Ausperk, Catherine, author.
Title: Hot-ticket meetings / Catherine Hakala-Ausperk.
Description: Chicago : ALA Editions, 2020. | Series: Leadership planners series | Includes bibliographical references. | Summary: "This succinct Leadership Planner is loaded with self-reflective questions, activities, and prompts that will help you turn meetings into the kind of hot-ticket gatherings that make attendees feel motivated, informed, and included"—Provided by publisher.
Identifiers: LCCN 2019027230 | ISBN 9780838946282 (paperback)
Subjects: LCSH: Library meetings. | Library meetings—Problems, exercises, etc.
Classification: LCC Z678.83 .H35 2019 | DDC 025.1—dc23
LC record available at https://lccn.loc.gov/2019027230

Book design by Alejandra Diaz in the Expo Serif Pro and Fira Sans typefaces.

♾ This paper meets the requirements of ANSI/NISO Z39.48-1992 (Permanence of Paper).

Printed in the United States of America
24 23 22 21 20   5 4 3 2 1

ALA Editions purchases fund advocacy, awareness, and accreditation programs for library professionals worldwide.

With thanks to my greatest supporters—my family.

Contents

Why Plan?   ix

Hot-Ticket Meetings... 1

Plan to Become Legendary.. 3

Plan to Fix the Right Stuff.. 6

Plan to Build a Virtual File.. 11

Plan to Aim at a Goal... 15

Plan Your Script... 18

Plan the Cast and Crew.. 22

Plan the Production... 25

Plan to Have an Impact.. 28

Let's Meet!.. 32

Sources   37

AUTHOR'S NOTE

There are more of these leadership planners in the works. You can help make each one better than the next! Please send your feedback, criticism, suggestions, and topic ideas to me. What kind of leadership success would you like to plan?

chakalaausperk@gmail.com

It wasn't raining
when Noah
built the ark.

—RICHARD CUSHING

Why Plan?

NO ONE PLANS TO FAIL BUT, ODDLY ENOUGH, FEW PEOPLE PLAN TO SUCCEED. Using the planners in this series, you can do just that.

Planners are making a comeback (if they ever really went away). Even though we have high-tech tools we can use to chart our lives, today's planners are bright and engaging. Why use them? There are as many answers as there are lines on which to write.

Planners, experts tell us, can help us to get and stay organized, make more intentional choices, be more productive, waste less time, reduce stress, and provide the time and tools that can help us solve today's challenges.

These planners are designed for library leaders who are facing some pretty serious challenges but haven't even had the chance to close their doors (if they have doors), sit back, untangle their issues, and begin to think about how to make things better.

Write in this book. Think of it as a combination to-do list, diary, and surrogate hairdresser or bartender (or any other good listener) that can provide you with the space, advice, and the luxury of time to think things through.

By the time you've finished the readings and exercises, you will not have solved your problems. But you will be ready to start solving them—and you'll have a plan to do so.

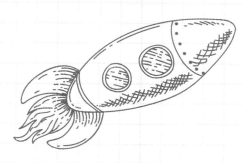

Somewhere, something
incredible is waiting
to be known.

—CARL SAGAN

Hot-Ticket Meetings

HAVE YOU HEARD (or used) any of these excuses in order to avoid attending a meeting? *I have to cover the desk. I'll let everyone else go. My garage door won't open. I need to get some work done. I have a doctor's appointment.* I have. I've actually gotten close to pulling out all the stops and using, *I have to rearrange my sock drawer* or *it's time to clean the crumbs out of my toaster oven.* Anything. *Anything* to avoid sitting through or leading another do-nothing, time-wasting, fingers-on-the-chalkboard, we-talk-about-the-same-thing-every-month meeting.

And yet we know, because we hear it all the time, that communication is the single most important key to a healthy culture and a productive workplace. And meetings are how we communicate. We need meetings. But the truth is, what we really need to do is to make them better.

This is not another "try using a timed agenda" book about meetings. This planner will introduce *real* changes. If you incorporate some of the suggestions from this planner, you'll be introducing significant innovations to how meetings are run and how information is shared in your organization.

What happens if nothing changes? What will the impact be to your organization if the meetings continue to be dull, pointless, and (of course) something to be avoided at all costs? In that case, you should probably get ready to hear the other excuses that come when meetings aren't the focus of a strong team. *I have no idea what's going on. Who knows what they're thinking? They don't even know what I do. Nothing will ever happen around here. No one upstairs cares what we really need.* Or worse—the all-too-frequent *they never tell me anything.* These are complex and destructive opinions that have a very simple remedy—hold outstanding, intentional, and effective meetings that people *want* to attend.

Yes, you heard me right. If you plan them properly, your meetings can become *the* place to be to feel confident, motivated, informed, and included. An invitation to a meeting like that would be a hot ticket, indeed.

Being a hero
doesn't mean you succeed
at saving the day.
It just means you tried.

—JAMES MARSTERS
(SPIKE FROM *BUFFY THE VAMPIRE SLAYER*)

Plan to Become Legendary

WHO DO YOU think of when you hear the word *legendary?* Ask most people and you'll hear names like Tarzan, Lady Godiva, and Elvis. Why? Because they were extraordinary people (be they real or fictitious). They changed lives. They got people's attention. They took risks. They were inspirational. They had an impact.

Although it could be considered a reach to compare Tarzan with a library leader, it's not impossible for a library leader to be legendary. Think about all the outstanding leaders you know and consider what makes them so special. We all know of (or, if we're lucky, we've worked with) bosses, managers, or directors who are famous for their courage, for their vision, and for the impact they've had. Think about it. In every aspect of our work, real leaders have led changes that mattered. Listen to some legends. It's time you heard about all of them.

If they can do it, so can you! You can take on meetings and turn them into something new and exciting. At the very least, you can greatly impact the lives of those you lead, and at most, you can help your library become much more successful at sharing information. Hot-ticket meetings require risks, as do almost any changes that make a true difference. This planner will break down how to host hot-ticket meetings into six distinct elements:

- ✓ Create and use a staff *Virtual File* (for all that information that can just be read).
- ✓ Clarify every meeting's *goal* (and make sure everyone knows it ahead of time).
- ✓ Design *scripts*, not old-fashioned agendas (because *scripts* direct action).
- ✓ Include the right *cast* and *crew* (and uninvite those who don't need to be there).
- ✓ *Produce* a successful event (but run the meeting, don't star in it).
- ✓ Assure *impact* (so because of your meeting, something will happen).

After you make these changes, you'll be hearing acceptances, not excuses, when you call your next meeting.

Living Legends

It's valuable to recognize and remember all the people you've known or heard about whose work, efforts, and ideas have made an incredible impact in your library, a neighboring library, or libraries in general. (I'll give you the first one: fill in the name of Nancy Perl next to "Readers' Advisory" and describe the risks, the changes, and her impact.) Complete this sheet using the names of national and local legends, or even the name of someone who sits right beside you. If you can't think of examples for each category in the following activity, ask around. Do some research. Recognize their work and then prepare to have your name added to this list.

	THE LEGEND	RISK THEY TOOK	WHAT CHANGED?	WHY ARE PEOPLE STILL TALKING ABOUT IT?
READERS' ADVISORY				
ACCESSIBILITY				
REFERENCE				
CIRCULATION				
FINANCE / BUDGETING				
COLLECTIONS				
TECHNICAL SERVICES				
STAFFING				
TECHNOLOGY				
PROGRAMMING				

You gotta stop
watering dead plants!

—UNKNOWN

Plan to Fix the Right Stuff

WHY FOCUS SPECIFICALLY on the six meeting elements—the Virtual File, goal, script, cast and crew, production, and impact? Because they need the most attention. If you begin with them, and innovation catches on, you and your team will likely come up with even more meeting enhancements on your own.

Oh, sure, we've all made attempts in the past to update our meetings. We've tried timing the agendas (which rarely works), and we've tried moving, changing, shortening, or lengthening the meeting time (which often only moves, changes, shortens, or lengthens the problem). And we've tried adding fun and even food (not a bad idea), but none of these attempts have really made much of a difference. Like the proverbial rearranging of deck chairs on the Titanic, all too often these adjustments just look new, but aren't necessarily better.

No, something big needs to change to truly make your meetings into events people won't want to miss. With this planner, you're going to concentrate on fixing the right things and getting the wrong things out of the way. By the end of this book, you're going to feel confident planning and conducting your first hot-ticket meeting. But none of the changes you'll be implementing will divert you and your team from what really actually needs to happen in a meeting. Even with all the things you will be doing differently, some important elements of a meeting will remain the same. For example,

- You *will* continue to make sure that people have access to everything they need to know (even if they're not all invited to attend each meeting, which they won't be). You'll accomplish this with your new staff Virtual File.
- You *will* make sure everyone knows *why* you're holding a meeting (because it's the second Tuesday of the month won't count). You'll accomplish this by identifying a clear goal for each event.
- You *will* make sure the right people come—and they come prepared to participate and contribute to achieving your goal. You'll accomplish this by inviting only those who really need to be there and sharing material they'll need to prepare for the meeting through the Virtual File.
- You *will* hold your meetings at the right place, at the right time, and through the right vehicle(s). You'll accomplish this by setting thoughtful, realistic schedules and by taking advantage of any technology you might need (for example, to create a virtual meeting room).

Admit it. There have been plenty of times when you walked out of a meeting thinking, "Well, that was three hours of my life that I'll never get back." You've probably managed to miss a few too, just to hold onto those hours. Why? What's been your beef? What are your top ten gripes about meetings? Start with the most minor and save number one for the worst. Getting it all off your chest will help you to realize why the work ahead of you is worth it.

TOP 10 REASONS I AVOID MEETINGS

10 _____

9 _____

8 _____

7 _____

6 _____

5 _____

4 _____

3 _____

2 _____

1 _____

While there's a lot that's right about how we currently run our meetings, there's also plenty that we can improve. Before you start considering these new ideas, remind yourself—and write down—*why* you should. When the topic for this planner was originally presented to me, I said I wouldn't write it. I just didn't think the world needed another "how to have a meeting" book. Then one day, I realized *why* I was avoiding meetings, and put together a list of what I thought was wrong. At that point, I was inspired, encouraged, and convinced that our meetings can be better. You must feel the same, or you wouldn't have picked up this planner. So, get ready to plan to succeed!

It might be comforting to know we're not alone in our critical assessment of most meetings. You've got your list of gripes; Eric Matson of *Fast Company* has his own list. You might see yourself in some of his examples of what he calls the seven most deadly meeting sins:

1. **People don't take meetings seriously.** You've seen it. They arrive late, leave early, and spend most of their time doodling. And don't you just hate it when someone strolls in late and the facilitator says, "Okay, let's back up and review so our new guest can get caught up." *You can plan to establish and enforce more respectful attendance expectations and guidelines for your meeting's cast and crew. And you won't be inviting the people who were bored and doodling because they probably didn't need to be there anyway.*

2. **Most meetings are too long.** There once was a director who decided his three-hour meetings were too long, so he shortened them—but left the agenda the same. So, guess what happened? Yep, the meetings went long anyway and really threw off schedules. And he still never got through an agenda. *You can plan scripts or agendas that fit real timetables and real schedules.*

3. **People wander off topic.** I know a librarian who used to pride himself on "filibustering" near the end of staff meetings by asking all kinds of irrelevant questions to delay the meeting's end so he wouldn't have to get back to work. *You can facilitate fearlessly to assure your meetings stay on track.*

4. **Nothing happens once the meeting ends.** Most meetings begin by reviewing what hasn't changed since the previous meeting. In other words, assignments were made, but rarely carried out. *But everyone at your meeting will be there for a reason and to make a very specific contribution. And, you'll assure that there will be an impact by requiring and supporting accountability from everyone.*

5. **People lie (or at least keep quiet).** You can ask "Does anyone have an opinion on this?" a hundred times, but often those opinions are only shared via whispers and complaints as attendees head back to their desks. *Your meetings can develop assignments and deadlines for which there will be real accountability.*

6. **Information and authority are often missing.** If you are bringing people together to make a decision, you better have the info and support they need to make that decision—and there should be someone in the room

with the authority to grant permission. *You can plan to bring things and people to your meetings that you actually need.*

7. **Meetings never get better. Nothing changes.** Aha! This is where your legendary impact can come in. Bad meetings are historical. They're expected. They're considered unavoidable. *You can plan meetings that are truly hot tickets for change.*

Leading real change isn't brain surgery. It basically requires the intention to stop doing something that didn't work and replace it with something that does.

Room for Improvement

Getting a sense of how your meetings are rated right now can help you in two ways. First, it can motivate you to see where change is needed and, second, it can help you assess the value of your changes later on. (Okay, three ways—you can identify what is working and leave that alone.) Think back to the last major staff meeting you attended (or led) and give it a score for each category under each dial. Assign a score from 0–10 and then explain the number you give in detail.

**Staff could review
pre-meeting information.**

The meeting had a clear goal.

Time was spent on the right stuff.

**The right people came—
and came prepared.**

The meeting was well run.

**The meeting resulted in action
and had an impact.**

The single biggest problem
in communication
is the illusion
that it has taken place.

—GEORGE BERNARD SHAW

Plan to Build a Virtual File

HOT-TICKET MEETINGS ARE all about goal, process, and action. They're not about one adult reading aloud information that a group of adults could have read to themselves. And yet, this describes many of our meetings, doesn't it? So, obviously, that stuff must go. One of the first major changes your team members will notice is that you've cut the fat out of your meetings by removing information they do need to know—but you don't have to explain it to them because they can read it for themselves. But where? In the new Virtual File you're going to create.

Step one in creating your hot-ticket meeting is to introduce your new Virtual File. It doesn't much matter where you put it (some teams would love it online, while others would prefer a bulletin board in the staff room or even a clipboard at the main desk). What's important is that you design it, locate it, and sustain it in a way that's easy to use. And it's important that you require it be used. A few guidelines wouldn't hurt either. For example, consider some of these options for making your Virtual File interesting, a team effort, and something that's going to be used.

- Use the creation of the Virtual File as a team activity and skill-building opportunity and spread around the assignments to design, create, and maintain it. You might even provide some people with training that will help them grow the necessary skills.
- Which of your team members are creative? Have them design a Virtual File that's easy to access and use. It will need to be organized so that meeting minutes, announcements, calendars, and policies will be easy to find, but we're not talking ten numbers to the right of the decimal here. Consider borrowing a previously created wheel, rather than reinventing your own. Searching Google is a good start—even if you don't find the right template, you'll certainly find some good ideas there.
- Someone needs to be accountable for making sure any material that everyone must read is included and accessible. How soon after a meeting must minutes be added? (Definitely consider a staff training event on how to write brief and relevant minutes.) When must schedules and locations of meetings be posted?
- And finally, build into all job descriptions the requirement that everyone must read, understand, and/or interact with all assigned information.

Don't be tempted to skip this part. If you're not the ultimate authority at your library, start by getting permission and support from whoever can put some teeth into this step. It won't work if information from your meetings is removed but isn't made available somewhere else. Put it in your Virtual File and make accessing and absorbing the information a required step.

Read or Discuss?

Since it's not possible to add hours to the day, we're still going to have to fit our meetings into the workday, maybe an hour, maybe two. So, in order to focus on our goal, we need to make the best use of that time by getting rid of those purely informational sections. Think back again to those recent—or memorable—meetings you've attended (or led) and fill in the general topics covered in those meetings under Column #1—"Meeting Topic." Were any of these things you could have read yourself or were they things that you needed to discuss? Put a check mark in the column that best describes how that information was shared. Then, in the final column, explain how that information should have been shared. What you're likely to find is that we spend an awful lot of precious meeting time simply reading aloud to one another. It's time that practice came to an end.

MEETING TOPIC	READ?	or	DISCUSS?	

What would your online Virtual File look like if you were designing it as a webpage that resembled a newspaper? Draw on the gridlines to create your own columns and boxes in which to enter what might be appropriate for your library to include. Should each department or branch have a news section? Could you use a calendar? Should there be a separate section for minutes? What about announcements for upcoming meetings with information about where and when they'll take place? Sketch out what your Virtual File might look like and then sit back and imagine (1) how helpful having all this information together in one place might be; (2) how much meeting time would be freed up if people could just read the information themselves; and (3) how you can make sure everyone will use it.

STAFF VIRTUAL FILE

Find purpose.
The means will follow.

—MAHATMA GANDHI

Plan to Aim at a Goal

IT DOESN'T TAKE long for even the greenest boss to realize that the old standby, "Because I told you so" doesn't work with grownups. Before introducing change, experimenting with a new service, or introducing a new process, the only strategy that really works is to start with *why*.

Changing the way you hold meetings will be no different. If you want to maximize interest (and you do), build excitement and motivation (again, yes), and make your meetings truly innovative and impactful (which is the whole point), what better way to start than by identifying a good reason for holding a meeting in the first place?

Ameet Ranadive agrees. In his review of Simon Sinek's book *Start with Why: How Great Leaders Inspire Everyone to Take Action*, he quotes Sinek's simple statement: "People don't buy what you do; they buy why you do it."

So, why do you have meetings right now? Because it's 9:00 a.m. on the second Tuesday of the month and that's when you've always had them? Because the boss said that managers must get together once a month? Because a meeting just seems like a good idea? Unfortunately, those aren't unusual answers. I know of a library that gathered about fifteen managers, supervisors, and administrators together every single month for a three-hour meeting, whether or not there was anything to talk about or that needed their attention. Did they call these meetings because staff had three hours of their lives they wanted to get rid of? Why did they do it? Because they always had.

Imagine the revolutionary approach of holding meetings only when you have something very specific to *accomplish*. (Note that didn't say something specific to *share*, because whatever that is would have been posted in your Virtual File.) That's right. No more "it's-time-for-our-monthly meetings." Hold *purposeful* meetings—call a meeting when there is a target, or a goal, or whatever you want to call it.

As a matter of fact, call it what it is. Imagine calling a "budget approval meeting" or a "staff day planning meeting." Right off the bat, those you invite (and we'll get to that soon) will know exactly what they're coming to do, and the meeting won't end until that action is accomplished or, at least, assigned a deadline. "The why," Sinek reminds us, "is [the] reason for being. And the why is why anyone should care."

Looking Ahead

Consider the coming twelve-month period and identify twelve very specific, goal-oriented meetings that will be important for your library. An "approve the budget meeting" would be one example—everyone needs one of those. If you can't think of twelve, then leave some empty. Those would be the meetings that, without a goal, you wouldn't hold to begin with.

Meeting	Meeting	Meeting
Meeting	Meeting	Meeting
Meeting	Meeting	Meeting
Meeting	Meeting	Meeting

A goal without a plan
is just a wish.

—ANTOINE DE SAINT-EXUPERY

Plan Your Script

BY THINKING IN terms of hosting a new production, rather than just holding a run-of-the-mill meeting, your agenda can become a script. In large part, the action will be controlled, and everyone present will attend because they have a specific role to play or contribution to make.

The first rule of creating that script is to start with a blank piece of paper. (All too often, meeting agendas are created by using last month's agenda, and just adding a few tweaks.) If you absolutely must create and use a template, then label it only with the headings "Clarify the Goal," "Meet the Goal," and "Learn Something New."

If your traditional meetings begin with each department head offering a report, leave that out. Remember, those reports will have already been posted in the Virtual File and any resulting questions will have been handled one-on-one. (But if issues arise that require more action than that, it looks like you have another goal for a specific meeting.) If your traditional agendas also include updates on projects, cross them out too. Instead, consider how you might use these three simple categories for the outline, script, or agenda of your new, hot-ticket meeting.

- **Clarify the Goal**—Remember *why* you're having the meeting and how important it is to get full participation from everyone. Sometimes, the *why* might be controversial (for example, when you're announcing the library will remove reference desks and go to a roving format), while at other times, the *why* will be more informational but just as important (for example, "We have two weeks to submit our new, reduced budget to the council, so today we make final cuts.") Be sure everyone comes prepared by sharing any pertinent background information ahead of time in the Virtual File.
- **Meet the Goal**—You'll find more on this in the upcoming section on planning a production, but for the purposes of your script, describe exactly what will happen in this section in as much or as little detail as suits your organizational culture. You might, for example, list "Review Options," "Analyze Solutions," "Make Decision," or "Assign Tasks."

- **Learn Something New**—Growth. It's a critical but all too often overlooked benefit of having a group of people come together away from their day-to-day workloads. Take advantage of opportunities to include some type of training, learning, or growth experience as a consistent part of your meetings. How? Share an article ahead of time and have someone lead a discussion. Review a recent incident and run an "after-action report" to see if it could be handled better next time. Hold a fun pop quiz about new team members' names or where certain keys or policies are located. Watch a TED Talk or brief webinar on a skill you all need to enhance. There are as many options as there are opportunities. Use them all!

Script Practice

Think of three dream meetings you'd like to have to address ongoing issues or resolve challenges. Name each, and then practice creating agendas or scripts for each by filling in each of the three categories.

MEETING NAME	MEETING NAME	MEETING NAME
CLARIFY THE GOAL	CLARIFY THE GOAL	CLARIFY THE GOAL
MEET THE GOAL	MEET THE GOAL	MEET THE GOAL
LEARN SOMETHING NEW	LEARN SOMETHING NEW	LEARN SOMETHING NEW

Be a Learning Library

There are plenty of reasons and resources available to use when you have a room full of team members who have some time to learn. And, that's everyone, right? On each book, first write down a skill or ability you could focus on. Then, under each book, find a webinar, book, or other resource you could use to add a little learning.

Hard work
without talent is a shame,
but talent without hard work
is a tragedy.

—ROBERT HALF

Plan the Cast and Crew

WE'VE ALL SEEN this before: about half the people in the room are listening; some are focused on their phones or tablets, purportedly taking notes but really checking email or shopping; a few are talking to one another (they always do that!); some are just practicing their eye-rolling technique; and one guy over there is sleeping. And snoring.

Ask yourself why this happens. There are probably a lot of reasons. Maybe the topic doesn't apply to everyone. Have you ever seen shipping clerks sitting through a discussion of waiving fines? It's not part of their job—but they're members of the circulation staff, so there they are. And, even though this is the managers' meeting, shouldn't all the managers care about each topic? (No.) But they all work here so they all want to be active participants in the big picture of the organization? (No again. And that's okay.)

So how do you keep all meeting attendees focused—and awake? Easy. You invite the right people and let the others read about it in the minutes.

This is probably one of the most revolutionary changes you'll make in moving to hot-ticket meetings. No longer will a Summer Reading planning meeting involve every single member of the children's staff. And, no longer will your monthly managers' meeting involve every single supervisor in the system. Instead, you will be inviting only those who need to be there to each meeting, depending on the goal. No longer will everyone with the same title or pay grade be seated around the table but, instead, everyone who is directly related to or will impact your goal will be coming.

For each meeting, you'll be putting together an ad hoc group of creative, experienced, and (most important) motivated team members who are affected by and/or who can impact the goal at hand. These are the people who will get the job done. Remember to prepare them ahead of time by sharing any background information they'll need in your Virtual File (and requiring them to read it). Then, you'll proceed through your script by clarifying the goal, accomplishing it, and learning something new along the way.

And, don't be afraid of not compiling the perfect invitation list. Anyone with something to add who really wants to attend will let you know. Wouldn't that be a positive twist? People *asking* to come to a meeting?

One more thing: be sure to have a dependable crew on hand to handle technical details. Nothing is more frustrating than bringing people together to watch a video or to trying to bring many locations together for a virtual meeting only to find that the settings aren't right. Plan ahead and make sure everyone you need is there. Remember, your meetings are now hot tickets because they don't waste time or energy—they actually get things done.

Six Hats

If you get the right people to a meeting, how can you make sure they each have the opportunity to participate? How can you be sure that the unique knowledge or experience they bring is as well used as their time? Here's one possibility to try out. As suggested in *Transform and Thrive* (Stoltz), consider using Edward de Bono's "Six Thinking Hats" design. With this model, everyone is given a different "assignment." These can be switched and shared, giving everyone a chance to stretch and use different skills. Imagine a real meeting you might host and list real people from your team (or even outside your library) whom you would invite. Put each person into one of these roles and explain what they might contribute to your discussions.

WHITE HAT
What facts do I need and how do I get them?

RED HAT
How will everyone feel about this?

BLACK HAT
What are the risks and worst-case scenarios?

_____

_____

_____

YELLOW HAT
What are the potential benefits and best-case scenarios?

GREEN HAT
What ideas does this generate?

BLUE HAT
What's the next step?

_____

_____

_____

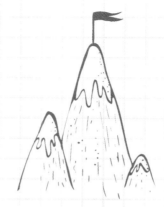

Whether you think you can,
or you think you can't,
you're right.

—HENRY FORD

Plan the Production

BY NOW, YOU'VE gotten everyone's attention. You've created a new Virtual File and required that it be used effectively. You've limited attendance at your meetings to only those who can contribute, and you've changed your traditional script or agenda into a list of three topics. Everyone's assembled, waiting for you to continue to wow, inform, or aggravate them, as the case may be. Now it's up to you to run the meeting effectively. You can do this.

One way to prepare to produce a successful meeting is to remember what it's like to attend one that wasn't. You've already attacked most of Joel Levitt's seven symptoms of bad meetings, but review them anyway, just to reaffirm what you're not going to do.

1. **Most meetings ramble on without a clear purpose and if there's an agenda, no one follows it.** This won't happen in your meetings because your goal will be clear, and your meeting will focus only on it.
2. **People drift off and do their own thing during the meeting.** Nope. Your audience will have been invited for a reason—and will have a purpose for being in the room.
3. **People show up who are not prepared.** Not with a Virtual File, they don't.
4. **There's no closure for decision making.** Remember your outline (or agenda). In only three steps, you're going to clarify your goal, meet your goal, and then learn something new. That's closure!
5. **The wrong people talk or don't talk.** Wrong. The right people will be at your meetings—and they'll be there prepared to participate.
6. **Meetings start or end late.** Well-planned meetings don't.
7. **People leave tired, frustrated, angry, or depressed.** Your meetings wouldn't be hot tickets if that were true.

There are as many different ways to run a meeting—or direct a production—as there are how-to books on your shelves, so it doesn't do any good to pretend there's one perfect approach. All you can do is learn what you can, and then make it fit your library's reality.

Everything from your library's culture, from the speed at which change feels comfortable to the willingness of talented participants, will contribute to your success. But you, as the leader, matter a great deal, too. You need to plan carefully for things to go well and be prepared to fix them when they don't.

Staying on Track

Picture a meeting you're going to have soon, and for each of these potential problems or symptoms of a bad meeting, plan and describe real steps you will take to overcome them and keep your meeting on track.

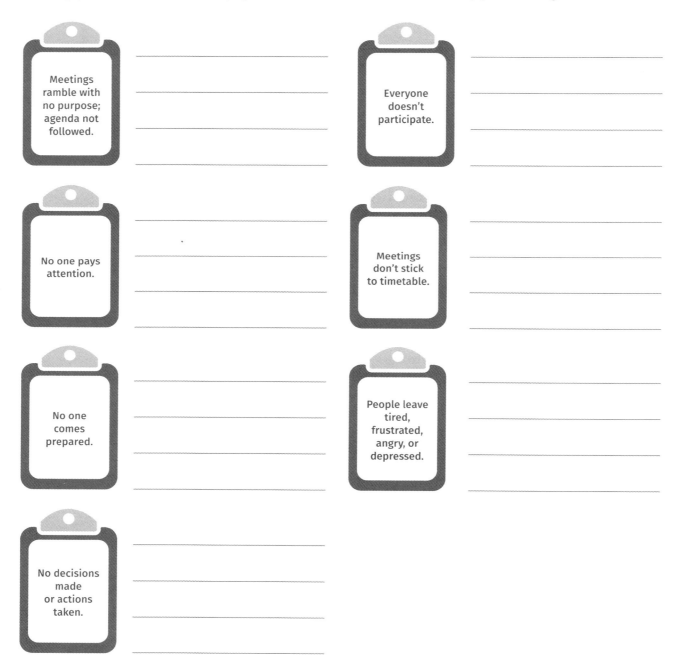

Meetings ramble with no purpose; agenda not followed.

Everyone doesn't participate.

No one pays attention.

Meetings don't stick to timetable.

No one comes prepared.

People leave tired, frustrated, angry, or depressed.

No decisions made or actions taken.

When you hand
good people possibility,
they do great things.

—BIZ STONE

Plan to Have an Impact

ONE OF THE standard measures I use and teach to determine the value of an interview question is not a complicated, high-level managerial tenet but a simple question: *So, what?* Before you ask a question, consider the likely answer you'll get, and then ask yourself, *So, what?* Will the answer help you learn anything of value? Will it tell you something about the candidate that you don't know? Do you even want to know it? What are the chances any answer you hear to this particular question will have an impact on your evaluation of the candidate or on your final decision?

The same could be said for all the potential changes you will be making to turn your organization's meetings into hot tickets. After clarifying the meeting's goal, inviting the right people, uninviting the wrong people, sharing material needed for the meeting in your Virtual File, creating a focused script to follow, and then directing a successful production, ask *So, what?*

The only way any of this will be worth it is if there's a resulting action or impact. Legends are created only when something happens or changes. Here's what you will change. Here's the *what?* in your *So what?*

- ✓ By creating and utilizing a well-organized Virtual File, you'll be eliminating gab sessions, redundant debates, and read-aloud reports that you all could have read on your own. You'll have freed up time to address the real issue—the goal at hand. You'll also be making sure everyone is prepared for your meetings, having read all applicable background information in the Virtual File beforehand.
- ✓ By establishing and clarifying the goal up front, and making sure it includes action, you'll be ensuring that something will take place. You may not save the world in an hour, but you can get started. Remember, even a walk around the world begins with the first step. If you are facing a large goal that clearly can't be achieved in one meeting, you can break off a piece of it and start by addressing that. Better to accomplish a part of something than none of something.
- ✓ By inviting the right people and uninviting the wrong ones to your meeting, you will be sure everyone will bring to the table the interest, experience, talent, and desire needed to make a real contribution.

✔ Your agendas or scripts will become second nature because they will consistently focus on just three steps: (1) clarify the goal (what, why, and with what action); (2) meet the goal; and (3) learn something.

✔ You'll run the meeting like a professional, focused production. Once people realize that their time will be well spent, they won't only be glad they came but will leave hoping to be invited again. You'll provide specific roles for each to play, which will ensure comprehensive input and broad idea sharing.

This is the impact you will have. Quite a change from the old, laborious, boring meetings everyone used to duck.

Ready? Action!

Impacts don't result by chance but by intentional actions. For each of these sample meetings, be more specific about the meeting's goal, then identify the action or impact that the meeting will achieve. There won't be any wandering in these meetings. You're going to achieve what you set out to do.

Your meeting has something to do with . . .	The specific meeting goal is to . . .	Action
Job descriptions	Begin the process of updating job descriptions	Who will do what and by when
Budget		
The levy		
Dress code		
Holiday party		
Student orientation		
Eating in the library		
Programming		
Weeding		
Next strategic plan		

WHAT COMES FIRST, GREAT MEETINGS OR GREAT CULTURE?

In a perfect world, a focused and intentional culture would develop and improve as your hot-ticket meetings become more commonplace. Because of your innovations in communication, characteristics like respect, flexibility, and accountability will flourish. You can help nurture these developments by taking some specific actions to enhance the workplace culture.

To Get Healthier

- **Encourage Creativity**—Greg Satell and coauthors tells us that "expertise is absolutely essential for producing top-notch creative work." That's why learning is such an important part of your meetings. Use that last third of each agenda, the "learn something new" part, to encourage growth in expertise and creativity will follow.
- **Accept Risk**—New doesn't always equal safe and, in fact, it rarely does. Unless we lead teams that are willing to step into the unknown based on calculated risk, nothing new (or improved) will ever result. The best way to encourage risk-taking is to accept and admit mistakes—even your own! Even if the initial feedback is negative, hold several hot-ticket meetings in order to demonstrate your commitment to positive change.
- **Welcome Ideas**—A company with over 2,000 employees once admitted that it received roughly three new ideas a year. Three. In total. And, worse, that they weren't sure they'd even looked into any of them to see if they were good. Robinson and Schroeder remind us that ideas are free and, often, encouraging them and then trying them out can both liberate your people and transform your organization. Ask for constructive suggestions from your team to continue to improve your meetings and, most importantly, give those ideas a try, too.
- **Give Away Credit, Keep Blame**—Change, especially change that shakes up tradition, doesn't always go well at first. If you really want to change the very core of your meetings, you may be faced both with failure and success. Give away the credit for those successes but keep the blame for what doesn't work for yourself. And fix it. And try again. Above all, keep going. There are lots of directions from which to choose. The best, to be sure, is forward.

Success results when preparation meets opportunity.

—ERMA BOMBECK

Let's Meet!

IT'S TIME. YOU'RE ready.

In this activity, you're going to lay out your script for your very first hot-ticket meeting. (You can come back to and use this template for future meetings, as well.)

Your very first step, though, is to be certain not to skip over the creation of your library's Virtual File. You probably already have the bones of some type of intranet that can be the basis for this resource. Whenever you build on it or create something from scratch, remember these very basic foundations to ensure your success:

- **Make your Virtual File widely and easily available to all.** Don't barricade it with complicated software or passwords worthy of the Pentagon. If possible, it should be accessible via an online blog or website or even Google Docs. Easy to find and easy to use should be the guideposts.
- **Put some teeth in it.** Require—don't request—that people use the Virtual File. Don't threaten banishment or public humiliation, but make sure there is some consequence for "I didn't know it was there," or "I didn't have time to read it."
- **Train.** Stand behind your Virtual File and make sure training to use it is in place and is easy to find and use.
- **Keep it simple.** One library used to charge a $10 fine (to be donated to the Friends) for any meeting minutes that exceeded one page. That might seem a little overboard—or not—depending again on your particular culture. Perhaps you can even let someone creative on your team develop a template for all minutes that reflects your three-part script: (1) clarify the goal, (2) achieve the goal, and (3) learn something new.

Directions

For this activity, first read through the descriptions below for each section of your script and then enter your answers in the matching section of the script on the following page. Complete one section at a time. Be real. Pick a real, actual hot-ticket meeting you intend to hold—and soon!

1. **Meeting Name** (*including time, place, and how to access, if virtual*)
    It's time to get everyone's attention. Don't start by calling a routine budget meeting. Plan your first hot-ticket meeting around something pressing and truly relevant. To be sure you're not wasting time on an irrelevant topic, use the problem-solution-opportunity approach:
    -   Think of a serious problem facing your team.
    -   What would the likely solution to that problem be?
    -   Find an opportunity to offer or take part in that solution. Now you have your meeting goal.

    ❯❯ *Enter your meeting name and date, time, link, and location in the appropriate line on the next page.*

2. **Cast** (*Whom will you invite?*)
    Because one of the biggest (and impactful) changes you will introduce will be choosing specific people to be invited to your meetings, be sure to stick to your guns with this one. Consider the goal and action intended, then decide who should be there. Your cast list will be broad and inclusive, perhaps even including some staff appropriate to the task who are not usually invited to such events.

    ❯❯ *Enter their names now under "Cast" in the appropriate line on the next page.*

3. **Crew** (*What kind of support will you need?*)
    Will you need help with technology? What about food? Who will set up the tables and chairs? List the team you'll need and be sure to clarify everyone's purpose or assignment.

    ❯❯ *Enter their names (and assignments) now under "Crew" in the appropriate line on the next page.*

4. **Prep Info** (*available in Virtual File*)
    You want everyone to come prepared, which might require them to do some reading and review some background information or minutes of previous meetings. Under "Prep Info," describe what attendees must read over beforehand. If possible, describe where in the Virtual File the material can be found.

    ❯❯ *Enter this information now under "Prep Info" in the appropriate line on the next page.*

5. **Clarify and Meet the Goal** (*Be sure to use an action verb.*)
    The most important part of your new script is to clarify your meeting's goal. This is an important way for you to identify opportunities for your attendees to be part of a particular solution. Under "Meeting Goal," state your goal clearly, using an action verb, to further illustrate that something will happen because of this meeting.
    Although you won't describe the process you plan to use to reach your goal here, this is a good time to consider options. Think about how you'll achieve the result you're aiming for. Will you be assigning a Six Hats approach or something similar? Maybe you'll split the group into a pros and cons debate? Or perhaps you'll want to go with a flip chart list of ideas to start the discussion? Be prepared. Have a plan.

    ❯❯ *Enter your actionable goal now under "Meeting Goal" in the appropriate line on the next page.*

6. **Time to Learn** (*In the future, facilitating this section can be assigned to attendees on a rotating basis.*)
    Start off strong! Find a brief, compelling TED Talk or YouTube video featuring something of real interest to your cast. Or share an article ahead of the meeting in your Virtual File to discuss. Pick something amazing. Pick something fun. Pick something that will make the meeting time set aside for learning both worthwhile and enjoyable.

    ❯❯ *Enter your topic and/or link now under "Time to Learn" in the appropriate line on the next page.*

Script

1 MEETING NAME

2 CAST

3 CREW

4 PREP INFO

5 CLARIFY AND MEET THE GOAL

6 TIME TO LEARN

You did it! Now you're ready to truly change the communication culture of your team. Keeping in mind that nothing exceptional is easy or can occur overnight, give some final thoughts to exactly *how* you'll go about introducing these new ideas.

HOW TO GET (AND KEEP) THE CONVERSATION GOING

Everyone invited to your meeting is there because she or he can bring something very specific to the table. You will need to hear from them all. Because there are always people who are reluctant to speak up in a group setting, some tips on getting everyone engaged in the discussion might be helpful.

The book *Game Storming* offers lots of enjoyable ways to get everyone talking in a meeting. One of the best is also one of the simplest. Ask questions! For example,

- How should this work?
- What are the pieces and parts of this process?
- What else works like this?
- What are we missing?
- What if all the barriers were removed?
- What if we go wrong?

Remember that there is one very important ground rule to make this approach truly effective: *There are no bad comments.*

One Step at a Time

Now that you've finished this planner, think about what you are going to do now. What steps do you need to take to put your plan into action? Do you need permission from a superior? Do you want to run the whole idea past a mentor first? Or do you want to jump right in and give it a try? As you fill out this final exercise, be realistic but challenge yourself to start taking steps *now* to incorporate hot-ticket meetings into your organization. Describe specifically, with days and dates and deadlines, what you will do *right away;* what you will do *very soon;* and, finally, what you will do *when the time is right.*

As promised at the beginning of this planner, although the problem of bad meetings at your organization isn't solved, you now have a plan to do so. Once the value, impact, and effectiveness of your new style becomes known, attendance at your events will become hot tickets indeed!

3

When the Time Is Right

2

Very Soon

1

Right Away

Sources

de Bono Group. "Six Thinking Hats." http://www.debonogroup.com/six_thinking_hats.php.

Gray, David, Sunni Brown, and James Macanufo. *Gamestorming: A Playbook for Innovators, Rulebreakers, and Changemakers*. Beijing: O'Reilly, 2010.

Matson, Eric. "The Seven Sins of Deadly Meetings." *Fast Company*. September 8, 2017. https://www.fastcompany.com/26726/seven-sins-deadly-meetings.

Ranadive, Ameet. "The Power of Starting with Why—Leadership" Medium.com. May 26, 2017. https://medium.com/leadership-motivation-and-impact/the-power-of-starting-with-why-f8e491392ef8.

Robinson, Alan, and Dean M. Schroeder. *Ideas Are Free: How the Idea Revolution Is Liberating People and Transforming Organizations*. Strawberry Hills, Australia: ReadHowYouWant, 2008.

Satell, Greg, Emma Seppala, Emma Schootstra, Dirk Deichmann, Evgenia Dolgova, and Priscilla Claman. "Set the Conditions for Anyone on Your Team to Be Creative." *Harvard Business Review*. December 07, 2018. https://hbr.org/2018/12/set-the-conditions-for-anyone-on-your-team-to-be-creative.

Sinek, Simon. *Start with Why: How Great Leaders Inspire Everyone to Take Action*. New York: Penguin, 2011.

"Seven Symptoms of Bad Meetings and What You Can Do About Them." Life Cycle Engineering. https://www.lce.com/Seven-Symptoms-of-Bad-Meetings-and-What-You-Can-Do-About-Them-1408.html.

Stoltz, Dorothy, Gail Griffith, James Kelly, Muffie Smith, and Lynn Wheeler. *Transform and Thrive: Ideas to Invigorate Your Library and Your Community*. Chicago: ALA Editions, 2018. Appendix B.

Notes